LIFE STORIES / BIOGRAFÍAS

FRANKLIN D. ROOSEVELT

Gillian Gosman

Traducción al español: Eduardo Alamán

PowerKiDS press

New York

Published in 2011 by The Rosen Publishing Group, Inc.
29 East 21st Street, New York, NY 10010

First Edition

Editor: Jennifer Way
Book Design: Ashley Burrell and Erica Clendening

Spanish translation: Eduardo Alamán

Photo Credits: Cover (main, background), pp. 15, 22 (top) George Skadding/Time & Life Pictures/ Getty Images; pp. 4–5, 6, 11 (bottom), 13 Hulton Archive/Getty Images; pp. 7, 12 Popperfoto/ Getty Images; p. 8 Transcendental Graphics/Getty Images; pp. 9, 16 FPG/Getty Images; p. 10 Topical Press Agency/Getty Images; pp. 11 (top), 14 MPI/Getty Images; p. 17 Fox Photos/Getty Images; pp. 18–19 U.S. Army Signal Corps/Time & Life Pictures/Getty Images; pp. 19 (inset), 22 (bottom) American Stock/Getty Images; pp. 20–21 Altrendo Travel/Getty Images.

Library of Congress Cataloging-in-Publication Data

Gosman, Gillian.
[Franklin D. Roosevelt. Spanish & English]
Franklin D. Roosevelt / by Gillian Gosman. — 1st ed.
    p. cm. — (Life stories = Biografías)
Includes index.
ISBN 978-1-4488-3222-4 (library binding)
1. Roosevelt, Franklin D. (Franklin Delano), 1882-1945—Juvenile literature. 2. Presidents— United States—Biography—Juvenile literature. 3. United States—History—1933-1945—Juvenile literature. I. Title.
E807.G67718 2011
973.917092—dc22
[B]

2010038440

Web Sites: Due to the changing nature of Internet links, PowerKids Press has developed an online list of Web sites related to the subject of this book. This site is updated regularly. Please use this link to access the list: www.powerkidslinks.com/life/fdr/

Manufactured in the United States of America
CPSIA Compliance Information: Batch #WW11PK: For Further Information contact Rosen Publishing, New York, New York at 1-800-237-9932

CONTENTS

CONTENIDO

Meet Franklin D. Roosevelt

In 1933, President Franklin D. Roosevelt gave his first fireside chat. This was a speech on the radio about the president's plans for the country. Every president since Roosevelt has given speeches like this.

Roosevelt was a man who wanted to try new ideas. He led America through the **Great Depression** and **World War II**. These were some of the hardest times the country had ever faced.

Roosevelt is the only U.S. president to serve more than two terms. He was reelected in 1936, 1940, and 1944.

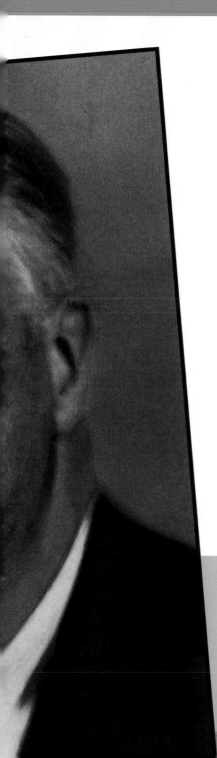

Conoce a Franklin D. Roosevelt

En 1933, el presidente Franklin D. Roosevelt dio su primer discurso junto a la chimenea. Éste fue un discurso en la radio en el que habló de sus planes como presidente para el país. Desde aquel día, todos los presidentes de los Estados Unidos han dado discursos como éste.

Roosevelt era un hombre que quería intentar nuevas ideas. Roosevelt condujo a los Estados Unidos a través de la **Gran Depresión** y la **Segunda Guerra Mundial**. Estos fueron algunos de los momentos más difíciles a los que se ha enfrentado el país.

Roosevelt es el único presidente de los Estados Unidos que ha servido más de dos mandatos. Roosevelt fue reelegido en 1936, 1940 y 1944.

YOUNG FRANKLIN

Franklin Delano Roosevelt was born in Hyde Park, New York, on January 30, 1882. His family was rich and well-known. Roosevelt went to Harvard University and then Columbia Law School. Roosevelt was a very good student. He passed the test to become a lawyer before he finished law school!

In 1905, he married Anna Eleanor Roosevelt. The Roosevelts would have six children, five of whom would live to be adults.

Here is Roosevelt with his mother (left), his daughter Anna (second from right), and two of his grandchildren.

Aquí vemos a Roosevelt con su madre (izquierda), su hija Anna (segunda a la izquierda) y dos de sus nietas.

Eleanor and Franklin were distant cousins. Eleanor's uncle was President Theodore Roosevelt.

Eleanor y Franklin eran primos lejanos. El presidente Theodore Roosevelt era tío de Eleanor.

Los primeros años

Franklin Delano Roosevelt nació en Hyde Park, Nueva York, el 30 de enero de 1882. Su familia era rica y bien conocida. Roosevelt fue a la Universidad de Harvard y a la Escuela de Derecho de Columbia. Roosevelt era muy buen estudiante. ¡Roosevelt pasó el examen de abogado antes de terminar la escuela de derecho! En 1905, Franklin Delano Roosevelt se casó con Anna Eleanor Roosevelt. Los Roosevelt tuvieron seis hijos, cinco de los cuales llegaron a la edad adulta.

Life During the Great Depression

Roosevelt became president during the Great Depression. On October 29, 1929, the **stock market** crashed. This caused many people and businesses to lose all of their money.

The Great Depression was the worst **economic** time in American history. As president, Roosevelt needed to help Americans and the economy.

During the Great Depression, soup kitchens fed many people.

Durante la Gran Depresión, los comedores populares alimentaron a muchas personas.

The day of the stock market crash became known as Black Tuesday because it was an unhappy day.

El día de la quiebra de la bolsa de valores fue un día muy triste que se conoce como el Martes Negro.

Vida durante la Gran Depresión

Roosevelt se convirtió en el presidente durante la Gran Depresión. El 29 de octubre de 1929, el **mercado de valores** se fue a la quiebra. La quiebra hizo que muchas personas y empresas perdieran todo su dinero.

La Gran Depresión fue el peor momento **económico** en la historia de los Estados Unidos. El presidente Roosevelt tuvo que ayudar a los estadounidenses y la economía.

THE YOUNG POLITICIAN

In 1910, Roosevelt was **elected** to the New York State Senate. In 1920, he ran as the Democratic **candidate** for vice president of the United States. He lost the election and left politics for a few years.

In 1921, Roosevelt caught polio. This illness left him **paralyzed** from the waist down. This meant that he would never walk again. In 1928 and again in 1930, Roosevelt was elected governor of New York.

Here is Roosevelt with James Cox in 1920 when they were running for president and vice president.

Aquí vemos a Roosevelt con James Cox, en 1920, durante su campaña a la presidencia y vicepresidencia.

This is a poster from when Cox and Roosevelt were running as Democratic candidates for president and vice president.

Éste es un póster de la campaña a la presidencia y vicepresidencia de Roosevelt y James Cox.

UN JOVEN POLÍTICO

En 1910, Roosevelt fue **elegido** para el Senado del estado de Nueva York. En 1920, participó como el **candidato** demócrata a la vicepresidente de los Estados Unidos. Roosevelt perdió las elecciones y dejo la vida política durante unos años.

En 1921, Roosevelt contrajo poliomielitis. Esta enfermedad lo dejo **paralizado** de la cintura hacia abajo. Roosevelt nunca volvería a caminar. En 1928, y nuevamente en 1930, Roosevelt fue elegido gobernador de Nueva York.

Roosevelt used a wheelchair because polio had left him unable to walk.

La polio obligó a que Roosevelt pasara el resto de su vida en una silla de ruedas.

President Roosevelt

In 1932, the United States was in the middle of the Great Depression. President Herbert Hoover, a Republican, was against starting programs to help people who were hurt by the Depression.

Roosevelt ran as the Democratic presidential candidate in 1932. He promised to begin programs to help the country recover from the Depression. Roosevelt won the election.

Here is Roosevelt during his 1932 run for president.

Aquí vemos a Roosevelt durante su campaña a la presidencia, en 1932.

Herbert Hoover lost the 1932 presidential election to Roosevelt.

Herbert Hoover perdió la elección presidencial de 1932 contra Roosevelt.

Presidente Roosevelt

En 1932, los Estados Unidos estaban en medio de la Gran Depresión. El presidente Herbert Hoover, del partido republicano, estaba en contra de poner en marcha programas para ayudar a las personas afectadas por la Gran Depresión.

En 1932, Roosevelt fue nominado como candidato demócrata a la presidencia. Roosevelt se comprometió a iniciar programas que ayudaran al país a salir de la depresión. Roosevelt ganó las elecciones.

The First Hundred Days

During his first 100 days as president, Roosevelt started many programs. These programs were known as the New Deal because they promised Americans a fresh start at life.

Roosevelt started programs that gave food, housing, and work to the people who needed it. He also passed laws that helped control the country's banking system.

Roosevelt's New Deal programs were meant to help people who were hurt by the Great Depression.

Los programas del Nuevo Trato de Roosevelt se diseñaron para ayudar a las personas afectadas por la Gran Depresión.

Roosevelt gave speeches called fireside chats. These speeches played on radio stations across the country.

Roosevelt dio discursos llamados "discursos de chimenea". Estos discursos se transmitían por la radio en todo el país.

LOS PRIMEROS CIEN DÍAS

Durante sus primeros 100 días como presidente, Roosevelt inició muchos programas. Estos programas se conocen como el Nuevo Trato, y prometían un nuevo comienzo para todos los estadounidenses. Roosevelt inició programas que dieron alimentación, vivienda y trabajo a toda la gente que lo necesitaba. También aprobó leyes que ayudaron a controlar el sistema bancario del país.

THE NEW DEAL

The New Deal is best known for its many projects. The Tennessee Valley Authority built dams across the South. This helped stop flooding and brought electricity to many places.

The Federal Writers' Project sent writers around the country to record stories and music from people. The Social Security Act gave money to people who were out of work and to older Americans.

The Civilian Conservation Corps was a New Deal program that gave people jobs in national parks and forests.

El Cuerpo de Conservación Civil fue un programa del Gran Trato que empleó a personas en los bosques y parques.

Here is Roosevelt speaking before a crowd in New York City in 1940.

Aquí vemos a Roosevelt, en 1940, hablando frente a una multitud en la ciudad de Nueva York.

El Nuevo Trato

El Nuevo Trato es conocido por sus numerosos proyectos. Por ejemplo, la Tennessee Valley Authority construyó presas en el sur del país. Estas presas ayudaron a evitar inundaciones y llevaron electricidad a muchos lugares.

El Proyecto Federal de Escritores envió escritores a todo el país para registrar las historias y la música de la gente. La Ley de Seguridad Social le dio dinero a personas que estaban sin trabajo y a estadounidenses ancianos.

THE PRESIDENT AT WAR

World War II began in Europe in 1939. On December 7, 1941, the Japanese navy attacked the U.S. **naval base** at Pearl Harbor, Hawaii. This attack drew the United States into the war.

The United States and the other **Allied nations** won the war. The war ended on September 2, 1945. Roosevelt would not live to see this day, though.

Here is Roosevelt with Winston Churchill (left) of Great Britain and Josef Stalin (right) of the Soviet Union.

Aquí vemos Roosevelt con Winston Churchill (izquierda) de la Gran Bretaña y Josef Stalin (derecha) de la Unión Sovietica.

Un presidente en guerra

La Segunda Guerra Mundial comenzó en Europa, en 1939. El 7 de diciembre de 1941, la marina japonesa atacó la **base naval** de EE.UU. en Pearl Harbor, Hawai. Este ataque metió a los Estados Unidos en la guerra.

Los Estados Unidos y las otras **naciones aliadas** ganaron la guerra. La guerra terminó el 2 de septiembre de 1945. Sin embargo, Roosevelt no viviría para ver ese día.

The attack on Pearl Harbor drew the United Statesd into World War II.

El ataque a Pearl Harbor llevó a los Estados Unidos a la Segunda Guerra Mundial.

19

An Early End

By 1944, Roosevelt was in bad health. He died on April 12, 1945.

Roosevelt led the country through the Great Depression and World War II. Some of the programs he started, such as Social Security, are still going today. He is widely thought of as one of America's greatest presidents.

This is the Roosevelt memorial in Washington, D.C. Roosevelt is shown with his dog, Fala.

THEY (WHO) SEEK TO ESTABLISH SYSTEMS OF GOVERNMENT BASED ON THE REGIMENTATION OF ALL HUMAN BEINGS BY A HANDFUL OF INDIVIDUAL RULERS... CALL THIS A NEW ORDER. IT IS NOT NEW AND IT IS NOT ORDER.

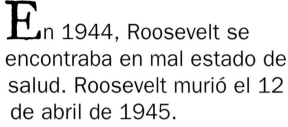

Un final prematuro

En 1944, Roosevelt se encontraba en mal estado de salud. Roosevelt murió el 12 de abril de 1945.

Roosevelt condujo al país durante la Gran Depresión y la Segunda Guerra Mundial. Algunos de los programas que comenzó, como el Seguro Social, aún existen. Roosevelt es considerado por muchos como uno de los grandes presidentes de Estados Unidos.

Éste es el monumento a Roosevelt en Washington, DC. Roosevelt aparece con su perro Fala.

Timeline / Cronología

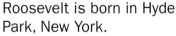

January 30, 1882
30 de enero de 1882

Roosevelt is born in Hyde Park, New York.

Roosevelt nace en Hyde Park, Nueva York.

1921

Roosevelt gets polio.

Roosevelt contrae polio.

1933–1945

Roosevelt is president. He is elected to four terms.

Roosevelt es elegido presidente. Roosevelt sirve cuatro turnos.

April 12, 1945
12 de abril de 1945

Roosevelt dies.

Roosevelt muere.

December 7, 1941
7 de diciembre de 1941

Japan attacks Pearl Harbor. The United States enters World War II, which lasts until 1945.

Japón ataca Pearl Harbor. Los Estados Unidos entran a la Segunda Guerra Mundial que dura hasta 1945.

1933

Roosevelt begins his New Deal plans.

Roosevelt comienza los planes para el Nuevo Trato.

Glossary

Allied nations (uh-LYD NAY-shunz) The countries that fought against Germany, Japan, and Italy in World War II. The Allies were Britain, China, France, the Soviet Union, and the United States.

candidate (KAN-dih-dayt) A person who runs in an election.

economic (eh-kuh-NAH-mik) Having to do with the production and supply and demands of goods and services.

elected (ee-LEK-tid) Picked for an office by voters.

Great Depression (GRAYT dih-PREH-shun) A period of American history during the late 1920s and early 1930s. Banks and businesses lost money and there were few jobs.

naval base (NAY-vul BAYS) A place where a country's navy houses its sailors and its ships.

paralyzed (PER-uh-lyzd) To have lost feeling or movement.

stock market (STOK MAR-ket) A market for buying shares, or part ownership, in companies.

World War II (WURLD WOR TOO) A war fought by the United States, Great Britain, France, China, and the Soviet Union against Germany, Japan, and Italy from 1939 to 1945.

Glosario

base naval (la) Un lugar donde se ubican las embarcaciones y los marineros de un país.

candidatos (los) Personas que participan en una elección.

economía (la) Relacionado con la producción y la oferta y demanda de bienes y servicios.

elegido Escogido por los votantes para un cargo.

Gran Depresión (la) Período de la historia estadounidense en la que los bancos y las empresas perdieron dinero y había pocas oportunidades de trabajo.

mercado de valores (el) Un mercado para la compra y venta de acciones.

naciones aliadas (las) Los países que lucharon juntos contra Alemania, Japón e Italia en la Segunda Guerra Mundial. Los aliados fueron Gran Bretaña, China, Francia, la Unión Soviética y los Estados Unidos.

paralizado Haber perdido sensibilidad o el movimiento.

Segunda Guerra Mundial (la) Guerra librada por los Estados Unidos, Gran Bretaña, Francia, China y la Unión Soviética contra Alemania, Japón e Italia, desde 1939 hasta 1945.

Index

Índice